Lithuania - Through the Wall

diary of a ten-day visit to my native land

Algimantas Kezys

D1592394

Loyola University Press   Chicago 60657

©1985 Algimantas Kezys

All rights reserved.

Printed in the United States of America.
Loyola University Press
3441 North Ashland Avenue
Chicago, Illinois 60657

Design by Aristarch Kirsch

Library of Congress Cataloging in Publication Data
Kezys, Algimantas.
Lithuania–Through the wall.

1. Lithuania—Description and travel.
2. Kezys, Algimantas.   I. Title.
DK511.L2K48 1985   914.7'504854   84-23388
ISBN 0-8294-0479-1

CONTENTS

INTRODUCTION

by Kazys Almenas

The eye, the lens, the memory, and time . . .

These are the standard filters through which we perceive the past in photographic journeys. In this book there is a fifth element too, and it is the darkest one of all.

It is the Wall.

Yes, it is the same Wall which slices through Berlin and cuts a mine-studded swath across the German countryside. There are no pictures of the Wall in this book. We are carried beyond it, deep into an occupied country. But its filtering power is strong. It determines first of all what we cannot see: the childhood home of Algimantas Kezys, the church where he was christened, the sights and moods of Lithuania that would surely be caught by his perceptive lens if he were free to wander the countryside.

He was not free to do so. Lithuania is an occupied country. Only certain narrow paths are laid out for those who make the effort and receive the permission to visit. Their time is limited. Ten days is, in fact, the maximum. A guide is provided. A bus. Some unobtrusive KGB operatives are assigned to watch from the background. Some promises are made. And most of them are broken.

The visit proceeds.

This, then, is the setting. It has to be kept in mind because once the pictures begin, this background is easily forgotten. After all, it has determined that which cannot be seen. It has restricted the choices, and the time.

But it has not restricted the imagination.

The first images we see through Kezys's memory and lens are those of history. This is not a simple matter of chronology. Lithuanians are a product of their history to a degree that is probably difficult for native Americans to comprehend. There is so much history; it is so varied, and above all, there is the constant fear that there might be just one more twist of history and we would join it ourselves. A vanished race, entombed in time. This has in fact happened to our sister nations, the old pagan Prussians and the Jotvingians. When we look back, we feel the cold breath of oblivion in the thirteenth century, in the seventeen century, in the nineteenth. Again in the spring of 1940 and in the fall of 1944, in most of the years that have followed. And we feel it now.

And so, at the beginning of his journey home Kezys steps back into history. He steps back as far as the chronicles will reach. Into the days of castles, and knights, and wars that were fought in a forest of lances. He steps into a time of pagans and crusades. Crusades undertaken not against the Saracens, but against the pagan Prussians, Jotvingians, Samogitians, and Lithuanians. It is a fact that for more than two hundred years Christian Europe sent its knights to fight these last pagans in its midst. Chaucer's gentle and courteous knight, for example, mentions that he fought against the Lithuanians. It sounds so quaint, so exotic, so remote now . . . But we were those pagans. The Prussians and Jotvingians lost. They are no more. Even the name of the ancient Prussians was appropriated by their Christian German conquerors.

But we survived, the Samogitians, the Lithuanians, and a remnant of the Jotvingians. We formed a state, built castles, organized armies, and wonder of wonders, we even ruled a major part of Eastern Europe for several hundred years. We became Christian in victory, not in defeat. The conversion lies between Kestutis and Vytautas. The father died a pagan; the son a Christian. We see their pictures on pages 8 and 9.

The old castles have largely crumbled. The faces of rulers with sonorous names like Gediminas, Vytautas, Algirdas, Kestutis, and Jogaila gaze mournfully at us from the pages of textbooks. Their achievements seem too remote and too great to have any application to our lives. If we are to learn a lesson from them, it is the lesson of survival. It is survival, after all, which enables Kezys to make the five hundred year leap from the stern bust of Vytautas to the gentle expression on the face of the Lithuanian Statue of Liberty.

This leap has spanned more than time and history; it includes our dream today for a democratic, self-governing Lithuania. We want to be part of the European community of nations. Our dream became reality sixty years ago only to become a dream again in the night of Soviet occupation.

This is a sketch of the history which frames the contents of this book. There are many other images within the picture. There are those which reach back to the Lithuania of Vytautas: the sole surviving gate of the city of Vilnius, the Renaissance halls and courtyards of its Jesuit university. A distant echo of the pagan past seems to remain in the deceptively simple figures of saints carved for wayside shrines by the folk artists.

There are images which came before the democratic Lithuania which is symbolized in the angel-like Statue of Liberty. The images might not be recognized by an outsider, but they are filled with historical meaning for a Lithuanian: the mother teaching her child, for example, when teaching was prohibited in Lithuania by the occupying Russian government; the humble cover of a Lithuanian grammar book published in Tilsit, Prussia in 1901. At that time books in Lithuanian were political statements by their very nature. They were outlawed and prohibited in Lithuania under the czars, and they had to be smuggled across the border. These are strong images together with the purposeful faces of our first modern writers.

Not all is history, of course. Kezys captures the landscape, the faces, and the human events which simply are today. A bus that does not start, a tipsy farmer on his way home, a child on a narrow country path, an old man weaving a basket. Life goes on. Indeed it must.

And yet even here history intrudes. In some pictures it enters brutally. This is our present story. One of the most painful images is the Church of St. Casimir in Vilnius (page 67). The church has been desecrated, and it is now an atheistic museum. By a poignant coincidence, 1984 marks the 500th anniversary of the death of St. Casimir, the only saint that the Lithuanians have. Which again is history. This is the price we paid for being the last pagans in Europe. And now his sanctuary is profaned by the oppressors.

We have come full circle. We are brought back to the Wall. The Wall which is not pictured in this book.

P R E F A C E

       Returning to Lithuania, I suppose, is decidedly different from most trips home. It is not just a matter of boarding a bus or hopping a plane to reach the place of one's birth. It is that, but it is also like climbing a forbidden wall. After you have climbed the wall, the rest of the trip is probably like most of the others—a curious rediscovery of an unforgettable world almost lost in one's memory, a nostalgic summing up of lifelong experiences, a realization of one's own past.

       I left my native Lithuania in 1944 when I was seventeen years old, and I returned there in 1983. I had not seen the country, its cities, its people, my relatives, or my sister Aldona for almost forty years.

       This picture story is an attempt to share the impressions of my trip home.

       While I was in Lithuania, I followed the prescribed route. Our group stayed in Vilnius, the capital of the country, for ten days. Most of the images in this book were taken there. But we were also taken on one day excursions to other cities—Kaunas, Druskininkai, Rumsiskes, Trakai, Anyksciai, and Niuronys. At the beginning of the tour we were promised that each of us would be granted permission to visit our own home town. But the permissions never came through. So this story of "going home" has to be told without pictures of my home in Vistytis and Kybartai, the towns where I was born and went to school as a child.

Algimantas Kezys

The Horizon

the landscape and horizon of Lithuania is undistinguished except for the occasional protrusion of an old castle here or a tall church there. The most famous protrusion is the old castle you see here which stands on a small hill in the city of Vilnius, the capitol of Lithuania, founded in 1387. The castle was built by Gediminas, the Grand Duke of Lithuania, in the fourteenth century. It has flown the flags of friend and foe alike. In recent years it has alternately flown the red flags of Hitler and Stalin.

Trakai, the fourteenth century island residence of Lithuania's Grand Duke

I went up this path and over this bridge to discover my roots. Step by step, plank by plank, I approached the castle of Trakai. There I was confronted by a brick wall and the entrance to the inner courts. Finally I entered the chambers of the past. This, like my mother's womb, was the place in which I was formed. My pride, my identity, my being are all associated with castles like this one, whether I have seen them in books, or in my imagination, or in reality.

one of my fellow travelers at Trakai castle

Trakai castle, inner court

Kaunas castle, fortification

Old structures often have eyes, mouths, noses. They have a life of their own, rich and varied, which includes the lives of those who built them, those who lived in them, and those who fought and died for them. These dead seem to live here forever.

sculpture in the historical museum of Trakai castle

All of our wars were holy, even those we fought against the armies wearing the cross of Christendom. These armies came from the West to convert us—Europe's last pagans—to the truth of the Catholic Church. We did not submit to the sword; we even won some of the battles. But we succumbed to the lures of Christianity after the marriage of our Duke Jogaila to the Polish princess Jadvyga. Now we are among the staunchest defenders of Catholicism, a nation engaged in a holy war against godlessness.

Two heroes of our past—Kestutis and his son Vytautas. Both are credited with making Lithuania a power in Europe in the fourteenth and fifteenth centuries. There were other rulers before them, and still others since, but only Vytautas is called "the Great." He extended Lithuania's borders from the Baltic Sea to the Black Sea, and finally defeated the Teutonic Knights at Grunwald in 1410. These victories tickle our pride even today.

Vytautas

armour of a Lithuanian warrior in Trakai museum

sculpture by Juozas Zikaras

Our "Statue of Liberty" now stands in a museum of sculpture and stained glass that was formerly the Army Church (Igulos) in Kaunas. The statue once stood on a high pedestal near the Museum of Liberation Wars. These wars were fought on three fronts during World War One—against the Russians, the Germans, and the Poles. We won, became independent, and erected this Statue of Liberty which, alas, survived on its pedestal for only twenty years. Its short-lived history reminds us that we are constantly torn between the East and the West. Our land is a bottleneck. Napoleon passed through it on his way to Russia, Hitler on his *Drang nach Osten,* and Stalin driving back the intruders. Being small and in the way of the mighty, we are constantly trampled.

Our Birthplaces

the village houses you will see here helped me and others on our tour to remember how our own houses looked when we were little children. These houses are now museum pieces, located in an outdoor museum of country life and made to look tidy. The houses we lived in were not so tidy. The dreams our parents dreamed were how to turn their shabby-looking cottages "red", that is, built with red brick and covered with red roof tiles.

country house in Niuronys

14

the house where the author Jonas Biliunas was born

the Ethnographic Museum of Country Life at Rumsiskes.   A primitive well (left), and a typical wayside shrine constructed by a local woodcarver (right)

Rumsiskes. Our unpretentious architecture

an old windmill at Rumsiskes

Carved entryways, like the one on the left, were status symbols in my remembered childhood. The ornamented and well-kept porch was a sign of the well-to-do. A plain entrance to an old house was a sign of the poor. Today, homes such as these are a common sight in Lithuania, even within the city of Vilnius.

rural home in Niuronys with the basic necessities—a well and mailboxes

22

an old house in Ukmerges Street in Vilnius

Behind plain windows such as these, there are always the traditional white lace curtains. And behind the curtains one can usually find the love, compassion, religion, warmth, and strength of family life.

23

The picture above shows the traditional wood and metal ornamentation at the entrance to the Museum of Forestry near Druskininkai. This museum was only opened within the last ten years.

Modern concrete ornamentation imitates the traditional wood scalloping of Lithuania. It decorates the entrance to a health resort in the town of Druskininkai.

City buildings, too, give examples of authentic folk art. Here we see a decorative metal collage which depicts some of the major buildings of the city of Kaunas.

The People

On my visit to my homeland, I looked for faces that might be classified as typically Lithuanian. Our facial structure does not seem to be very different from that of other East Europeans. We are probably less blond than the Swedes, less rugged-looking than the Germans, but more Western-looking than the Russians. Is there a distinct facial type that might be called purely Lithuanian? Probably not.

At first this basket maker looked like an ancient Lithuanian patriarch. But when I greeted him in Lithuanian, he did not respond. He was an outsider trying to make a living here; perhaps he was deported from his native land in Siberia or Mongolia and brought to this distant corner of the Russian empire called Lithuania. At that moment somehow I felt I understood his situation.

an employee at the Rumsiskes museum

Many Lithuanian people do not wish to be photographed. This lady was accompanying some American visitors through the Rumsiskes museum and seemed afraid that her picture might fall into the hands of unfriendly strangers.

a farmer in the village of Niuronys

This fellow had just come out of a local bar, and apparently he had had a few too many. He posed for this picture, climbed into his wagon, and went home. Horses provide the safest means of transportation when a driver is drunk. They have been known to bring their drivers safely home, even when the drivers were fast asleep. The government imposes strict penalties on people who drive cars after drinking.

This is the house where my family once lived in Vilnius, and this is my sister Aldona. Aldona never left the country during or after the war. We had not seen each other for forty years.

The house seemed somewhat diminished in size and less attractive than I had remembered it. In my memory the house was large and spacious and very well maintained.

Trakai castle

restored wall in Vilnius

This lady has just received a letter from the West! It could be from her son or perhaps from another member of her family who managed to get out before it was too late. Letters from the West are few and far between and carefully examined by the government. Visitors from the West are even less frequent or nonexistent. These people live their lives as best they can, as we do. But the sad thing is that we so seldom meet. We once belonged to the same family. Now we have become strangers—it is "we" and "they." Having said hello, we say good-bye, perhaps never to meet again.

A fellow traveler of mine from the
United States reads "Tiesa," a daily newspaper
published in Vilnius. The title of the newspaper
means "Truth"; the word is "Pravda" in Russian.
This particular fellow seemed to be skeptical about
dogmatic truth, especially if it was presented in
bold letters, as it is here. Is he chuckling behind the
paper? Is he angry? Perhaps he is only mildly
amused.

I will never forget our guide Raimonda. She was not only a lovely lady, but her spoken Lithuanian was music to my ears. Only we emmigrants from abroad can fully appreciate the treasure we have in our language. Having lived in foreign lands for so long, we have lost much of the finesse of our language. I usually hate guided tours—but not this one.

Niuronys

Old millstones like these would certainly be a rare sight along a road in the United States. The girls' whispered conversation reminded me of how the past is present for this generation in a way that it is not for those of us who now live in large cities.

This pleasant shopper was talkative from the first moment we met in this well-stocked store. He was a stranger to me, of course. I did not have a chance to say much to him. I just listened in amazement that I had found someone in present-day Lithuania who was not whispering when he spoke to a stranger. We parted in good spirits. But he never asked me for my name, nor asked where I came from. And I did not dare to ask him who he was. The people here seem to have learned how to communicate in pleasantries and to find out basic information by very circuitous routes. They have become experts in knowing how to read between the lines.

Produce from private sector farms is crucial to the economy; such farms far outproduce the collective farms. Here a happy vendor displays part of her fall harvest, and eager buyers scramble to purchase their winter stock of food.

near the Kaunas market

Probably not a sales transaction, but just a chance meeting of two old friends as one fortunate buyer carts away his precious goods. Merchandise is always scarce here. The people must be constantly on the alert for deliveries of goods and be prepared to stand in line for anything that might become available. The store clerks are abrupt to their customers. The buyers are almost beggars.

46

This bus in Trakai would not start, and the passengers volunteered to give it a push. Cars and trucks frequently break down in the Soviet Union. People learn to repair their own vehicles, to cope with the shortage of automotive parts, and to help one another. Men are often seen huddled over a car's engine or working together like this.

These youngsters seemed happy and carefree and harmless enough. They came up behind me and my sister, and one of them called out my name which he saw on the name tag of my camera bag. I turned around surprised and pleased that someone here knew my name. The young people invited me to join them, and I was eager to chat with them. But my sister pulled me by the sleeve and urged me to come along; she implied that we were in a hurry and had no time to talk with them. She never explained to me why she did that. I just had to assume that she knew what she was doing.

exit from the Museum of Forestry near Druskininkai

This is another picture of my sister Aldona. Can she see me? I spent ten days with her, and believe it or not, I did not have one chance to talk with her openly about what had happened to her after we were separated during the war. Aldona is a talkative person by nature; but during our time together she fell silent many times without any explanation. I, a visitor from the West, sensed the barriers that have been imposed on formerly open and outgoing people.

path in the Ethnographic Museum of Country Life in Rumsiskes

Lithuanians, like this girl, step carefully on prescribed paths, attempting to go forward, gingerly balancing modern styles with ancient customs.

detail of wooden sculpture in the Museum of Forestry near Druskininkai

Everyone in Luthania is conscious of ever-watchful eyes. And so we seek the peacefulness of forest spirits. Pagan Lithuanians once worshiped gods who resided in the trees. We still respect our forests.

side entrance, Cathedral of Kaunas

This old lady is probably just what she appears to be—an old woman on crutches at the entrance to a church. But one becomes so suspicious. Might she be an informant with sensitive microphones in her bag?

Nevertheless, we are usually a cheerful people, finding happiness wherever we can. This man is a relative who came to see my roommate Kazys at the *Lietuva* hotel in Vilnius.

outside Ciurlionis Art Gallery in Kaunas

Lithuania is a singing nation. We love to sing. The songs that have been imposed upon us from the East are, I suppose, well established now. They are based upon our old folk songs, with new words added. But the songs which have filtered in from the West are like forbidden fruit, they are eagerly sought and sung—the beauty of our folk songs notwithstanding.

modern sculpture in the recently-completed residential district of Zirmunai, a section of Vilnius

Our Beethovens and Tchaikovskys are yet to come; but we Lithuanians love to sing our old folk songs. We have lullabies; we have songs for mourning the dead; and we make love singing.

backyard in Vilnius

This is Rasa, my fellow traveller from Chicago. I photographed her here in Vilnius. Two months after our trip, Rasa got married and moved to the Bahamas.

Kazys Martinkus in front of "The Sun in the Falls" sculpture by Lalla Pullinen in the Helsinki airport

Here is Kazys, my roommate and fellow traveler from New York. I photographed him in the Helsinki airport just before we boarded our plane for Moscow on our way to Vilnius. Four months after returning from our trip, Kazys died of a brain tumor.

We are a Praying Nation

I was deeply moved throughout my trip by the deep religious spirit of the oppressed people in Lithuania.

"Our Lady of Sorrows" sculpture in the Folk Art Museum in Vilnius

Wood carvings, like this pieta, could once be seen everywhere in Lithuania, usually carved by the handyman next door. No one thought then that a simple statue like this would wind up one day on the shelf of a museum. This wooden icon shows the scars of weathering. It is a sign of great faith, simple and powerful at the same time. Figures like these are greatly treasured by people who in their sophistication may not be able to come down to such humble perfection.

sculptures in the Ciurlionis Art Gallery in Kaunas

The Enthnographic Museum of Country
Life shows some of our romantic past. A not-so-
distant past, however, for I still remember it.
Chapels, churches, and wayside crosses were once
an accepted part of our everyday existence. It does
not really matter whether we talk about our pagan
past, our Christian Middle Ages, or our atheistic
present; a place of worship is at the very center of
our humanity, even when it is empty.

The building you see here is called *Perkuno Namai*—the house of the Thunder God. It is clearly a pagan name. The fifteenth century Gothic brickwork shows the quality of local masonry. The building was originally constructed to house the commercial activities of traders. Later it became part of the Jesuit university complex. And today it houses a branch of the Kaunas historical museum. Even after all these years and function changes, the building is still referred to by its pagan title.

Here is the organ in the Cathedral of Kaunas. And on the right is the interior of St. Ann's Church in Vilnius. St. Ann's is a tiny building, a miniature church; and legend has it that Napoleon wanted to place St. Ann's in the palm of his hand and take it with him to Paris.

The Cathedral of Vilnius and its bell
tower were built in the late eighteenth century.
This beautiful building now houses a picture
gallery and a concert hall.

66

St. Casimir is the patron saint of Lithuania. Symbolically, the Soviets chose his church to house their Museum of Atheism.

Jesuit church in Kaunas

They say that this noble building has nothing in it today but an unused basketball court.

An old city gate in Vilnius known as *Ausros Vartai,* the Gates of Dawn. This formidable structure was once part of the city wall erected for the defense of Vilnius. It now serves as a chapel in honor of Our Lady. It is the major shrine dedicated to Mary in Lithuania.

In spite of possible retribution, people recite the rosary, publicly and out loud. They climb the stairs to the shrines on their knees, as this lady is doing at *Ausros Vartai* in Vilnius. And they enjoy the Latin language in their liturgies. Their prayers come from their hearts; their very souls seem to cry out when they pray.

Our Lady's shrine at the Church of St. Raphael in Vilnius

My sister Aldona met me at the airport in Vilnius and stayed with me throughout my ten-day visit. Her faith colored my whole sojourn in Lithuania. One of the first things we did together was visit this statue. We seldom passed a church without going in to say a prayer.

Folk Art Museum, Vilnius

Devotion to Mary provides the people with hope and comfort in these difficult times. This queenly Mary seems to embrace the simple people who now so courageously cling to their beliefs.

a sorrowful Christ

The typical image of Jesus that could be found in folk shrines and wayside crosses all over Lithuania was a seated, worrying Christ rather than a crucified figure.

Toward Learning and Achievement

the campus of the University of Vilnius

Founded by the Jesuits in 1579, the University of Vilnius was recently renamed in honor of a hero of the Soviet government. The Soviets celebrated the university's four hundreth anniversary, claiming it as the oldest such institution in the Soviet Union.

entering the university incognito

I like to think of the leg entering this picture on the right side as me, a Jesuit, entering the university that the order founded four hundred years ago. Jesuits are not allowed to teach here now. As is the case with all religious orders, the Jesuits are outlawed under the present regime in Lithuania.

Established in 1753 and is said to be the oldest astronomy institute in Europe.

observatory of the university of Vilnius

the main library of the university

Unlike university libraries in the West, there are no photocopying machines for the use of the students here.

This painting on the ceiling of the main library of the university shows a group of early Jesuits under the protection of the Virgin Mary with the Risen Christ and God the Father. The current directors of the university were kind enough to leave this picture intact. Our guide told us that the University of Vilnius was founded by the Jesuits four hundred years ago. The university has survived wars, occupations, and deportations, and still stands firm under different leadership. I did not tell her that I was a Jesuit priest.

St. John's Church, built in the baroque style of the eighteenth century, is part of the university complex. Its roofline is adorned with wrought iron crosses, Lithuanian folk art variations on an international architectural style. The church is now used as the university's Museum of Science, and it also displays the publications of the university press.

83

From 1865 to 1905 books printed in Lithuanian were forbidden by the Russian czar. The education of children in the Lithuanian language was done secretly by mothers at home. The perseverance of our mothers and the cleverness of those who smuggled books across our borders is a lasting testament to the determination of our people. We have come a long way.

A young mother was helping her daughter with her homework at the foot of the old castle in Kaunas. Even my picture-taking seemed an intrusion on their concentration. Although mothers no longer work at home at spinning wheels, families again bear the responsibility for teaching their children the Lithuanian language and the true history of their country.

exhibit in the Trakai castle museum

Speaking of our language, Lithuanian is an ancient Indo-European language related to Sanskrit. The grammar book you see pictured above was published in Prussia in 1901 when the printing of books in the Latin alphabet was forbidden in our country.

exhibit in the Trakai castle museum

Here are some books and periodicals published during the short period of Lithuania's independence between the two world wars. Creative use of the language flourished during that time.

Motiejus Valancius (1801–1875),
bishop, author, and historian

Kristijonas Donelaitis (1714–1780),
pastor and poet

There were no professional writers among our early literary figures. For the most part they were priests, doctors, or housewives who combined their careers with the founding of our national literature.

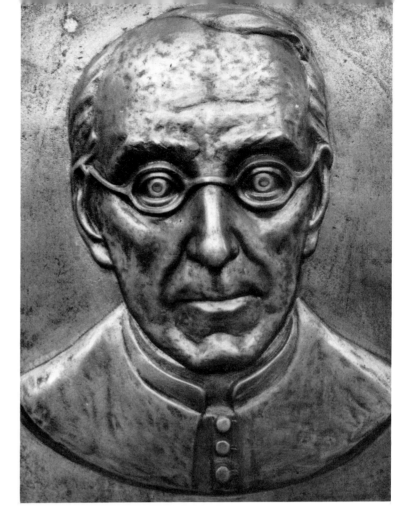

Julija Beniuseviciute–Zymantas (Zemaite) (1845–1921),
farm wife and novelist

Adomas Dambrauskas–Jakstas (1860–1938),
priest and literary critic

Mikalojus Konstantinas Ciurlionis (1875-1911) is our most illustrious painter and composer. There is a theory that he was a forerunner of abstract art in Europe.

This is Ciurlionis's home and art studio in Druskininkai which is maintained there as a museum.

The largest rock in Lithuania, is affectionately called *Puntukas*. It stands near Anyksciai, a lonely reminder of the glacial age that scooped and smoothed our country. It is truly a curiosity in a land of gently rolling hills.

Darius and Girenas were two Lithuanian pilots who flew across the Atlantic ocean from New York in 1933 and crashed in Germany minutes before reaching their destination in Kaunas. They are national heroes whose images are engraved here. This monument was dedicated in 1943 to commemorate their ill-fated flight.

93

The Farewell

Goodbye to old city streets

To the history-laden walls of churches and castles

A last glimpse of the University in Vilnius

— and my childhood school

A nostalgic goodbye to our romantic woods

—and farms

To the rivers Neris and Vilnele, goodbye

To our father-river Nemunas, farewell

Farewell once more to the dead

and to our homeland, perhaps never to return again.